# God is My Witness

## BY ROBERT SANDBERG

# God is My Witness

## BY ROBERT SANDBERG

CEDAR FORGE PRESS • SEATTLE, WA

All biblical references are taken from the Ryrie Study Bible, unless otherwise noted.

An *Original* Publication of Cedar Forge Press
PO Box 2222, Poulsbo WA 98370

Copyright © 2010 by Robert Sandberg

First Cedar Forge Press trade paperback printing
January 2011
10 9 8 7 6 5 4 3 2 1

ISBN 978-1-936672-02-8

Printed in the U.S.A.

# INTRODUCTION

## The Life of an Army Soldier

This is the story of my life in the U. S. Army and of our lives together (Ruth's and mine) after my discharge from the Army. The facts are true.

As you read this story, you will probably remember times in your life when you have experienced something beyond your power that has controlled your life. Maybe the way God has directed my life as a soldier and our lives as missionaries will encourage you to "trust in the Lord with all your heart, and do not lean on your own understanding. In all your ways acknowledge Him, and He will make your paths straight" (Proverbs 3:5–6).

# God is My Witness

BY ROBERT SANDBERG

## THE ARMY

## – 1 –

# Signing Up for the Army

*"...before they call, I will answer..."* (Isaiah 65:24a)

Upon graduating from high school in 1943, I was hired by the Seattle District of the Corps of Engineers for their Accounting Department. One day in November, during a coffee break, I happened to walk by the Army recruiting office—a day that would change the rest of my life.

A tall, burly sergeant sat behind a large oak desk, his shoes resting on the desk. "Ya wanta join up?" he asked as he lowered his feet to the floor.

"Been thinkin' 'bout it."

"Whacha interested in?" was his next question.

"I like horses; how 'bout the Cavalry?"

"Cavalry don't ride horses no more, they ride big steel tanks."

"Don't think I'd like that. What would you suggest?"

"If I was you, I'd join the Army Air Corps."

"Where do I sign?"

I walked back to the office and told my boss I'd just signed up for the Army. He wasn't very happy but had me signed out, and I was on my way home to say my good-byes and sell my car.

– 2 –

## Reporting for Duty

The next Monday I reported to Fort Lewis, and from there I was shipped off to St. Petersburg, Florida, for basic training and a lot of tests to determine where I was best suited.

I scored high on mechanics and office, so I was assigned to a school to learn how to repair airplane engines. I could see myself in some 120-degree desert working on engines, so I requested I be sent to Colorado State College to learn to fill out the paperwork required by the army. To my surprise, my request was granted.

After six weeks of intensive training at Colorado State College, learning how to fill out the mountains of paperwork required by the Air Corps, I was sent to Kerns, Utah, the most desolate place on this earth. I didn't know anything about the Bible, but as I look back, I can see God's hand was already guiding my life: "...before they call I will answer..." (Isaiah 65:24), "...and we know that all things work together for good to those who love God, to those who are called according to His purpose" (Romans 8:28).

Sundays, we were free, and a bus would take us to

Salt Lake City. So this particular Sunday, I decided to see the city. The entire day was messed up. When I awoke, the sun was shining, and the day promised to be beautiful. By eleven, a dust storm hit that blew dust two feet high between our barracks. By two in the afternoon, a snow storm hit that covered the entire place with two inches of beautiful, white snow, so the streets all around our barracks were slippery.

There were only a few stores open. I checked them out but didn't buy anything. As I sloshed along, I spotted a USO Canteen open. I was so cold, I decided to get a cup of coffee and a donut. As I stepped inside, another soldier spotted me and came over to welcome me. "By the way, do you bunk in T-41 back at camp?" he asked.

"I do. Why?"

"I think your bunk is the top bunk above me. Let's check when we get back."

During the week, we are busy from dark when we get up till dark when we go to bed; we don't have time to get to know anyone.

When we got back to camp, we realized we were bunk buddies. "My name is Bob Page. I'm from Minneapolis."

I laughed and said, "My name is Bob, too—Bob Sandberg. I'm from Seattle."

"Instead of going to town on Sundays, would you like to join me in Bible study?"

"Why not? There's not much to do in town Sundays, so I might as well join you. At least there's somebody here I can get to know."

It was through the Bible studies we had together that I came to put my trust in Jesus Christ. I had no idea how that encounter would change my life.

Through Bob's guidance, I learned several scriptures: John 3:16: "For God so loved the world, that He gave His only begotten Son that whoever believes in Him should not perish but have eternal life."

Romans 3:23: "For all have sinned and fall short of the glory of God."

Romans 6:23: "For the wages of sin is death, but the free gift of God is eternal life in Jesus Christ our Lord."

1 John 1:8–10: "If we say that we have no sin, we are deceiving ourselves and the truth is not in us. If we confess our sins, He is faithful and righteous to forgive us our sins and to cleanse us from all unrighteousness. If we say that we have not sinned, we make Him a liar, and His word is not in us."

These and other scriptures made sense to me, so I bowed my head and accepted that Christ died for me, and I accepted Him as my personal savior.

I had not read Isaiah 65:24, but I was soon to learn that scripture applied to me.

It was toward the end of our training. The bugler's loud trumpet call one morning got me out of bed. As I put my feet on the floor, I realized my right foot was swollen. It didn't hurt, but I couldn't get my shoe on.

"Bob, could you help me? Something's wrong with my right foot."

Bob helped me to the clinic. The doctor examined my foot but couldn't see anything wrong with it. He told me to stay in my bunk with my foot elevated until he released me. The doctor gave me a slipper to wear so I could get to the bathroom and mess hall. My foot didn't hurt. I could walk on it, but I couldn't put on my shoe.

Bob helped me to the mess hall for breakfast and back to my barracks. He handed an order from the doctor to the officer in charge of me, that I was to be excused from all duties until further notice.

Bob had given me a Bible, so I spent my days reading and keeping the small stove in the center of the building stoked with coal. The weather outside was extremely cold. The barracks weren't built with insulation, so it wasn't very warm even with the stove going full blast, but I had a warm wool blanket.

No one had a radio, and TV's weren't known. Day after day, I lay there with my foot swollen. About a week later, names were posted on the bulletin board listing the men who would be shipped out. The first list was for Africa. Bob's and my name were on it, but both of our names were deleted.

Several days later, another Army list was posted for Europe. Bob's and my name weren't on that list.

"I sure hope we get shipped out together," I commented. We had become such close friends.

Several days later, another list was posted for Alaska, and Bob's name was on it. The doctor had not released me, so I didn't know what was in store for me. If the doctor couldn't diagnose my problem, I supposed I would have to be released from the Army.

The next day Bob got his orders to ship out—a sad day for both of us. I felt so alone as I saw the bus disappear in a cloud of dust.

For a long time we did correspond, but we finally grew apart and our letters stopped.

The next morning when the bugler called, I noticed my foot was back to normal, so I put on both shoes and walked to the clinic. The doctor shook his head and said in a puzzled voice, "I don't know what was wrong with your foot, but it seems OK now. I am releasing you back to duty."

— 3 —

# On to Hawaii

The next day another list was posted, and my name was on it—to the South Pacific.

My next stop was San Francisco to a port of departure. Early the next morning, we were shuttled aboard the luxury liner Lurline. I suppose because we were members of the Army Air Corps, we were assigned state rooms complete with clean sheets. The Infantry had to bunk on the open deck.

I learned something about human nature. We didn't leave the dock until seven in the morning. However, at six in the morning, someone said we were on our way. Men were lined up in the bathrooms vomiting from being seasick. We were still tethered to the dock.

The trip was like a vacation trip, and I enjoyed every minute of it. I loved being on deck, watching the flying fish as they glided across the water. The trip took a lot longer than normal because we had to zigzag every seven minutes to avoid any enemy submarines. We traveled all alone—no escort ships.

One day I was on the bridge with one of the Naval officers. "If you were out in the ocean in a small boat," he said, "and you didn't have a compass, but you had a watch with hour hands, how would you find North?"

The entire trip a cormorant flew alongside the ship during the day, but it would rest in the rigging at night.

"Find a cormorant and follow it?" I said, jokingly.

"Take out your watch, point the hour hand toward the sun. Halfway between the hour hand and twelve o'clock is south." He took out his watch and showed me. "Of course, south of the Equator, it is reversed."

While aboard ship, we were given our orders. I was assigned to Headquarters Seventh Fighter Command. As soon as we landed in Honolulu, we were put aboard the "Tunnerville Trolley," a train used for transporting pineapples, headed for Wheeler Field.

As soon as I was assigned quarters (a single bed in a large room on the top floor of a large barracks), I dumped my duffel bag on my bed and headed for the airfield. A fighter pilot was just getting into an A-6 Fighter Trainer, so I asked if I could go with him.

*Bob, still wet behind the ears, poses in Hawaii, while stationed there with the Army Air Corps 37th Fighter Squadron.*

"Hop in and fasten

your harness!" he commanded. I'm sure glad I did. We shot almost straight up, then he did several barrel rolls, dove straight down, then performed a couple of loops. By this time, I was vomiting in the relief tube; I was airsick. I never got seasick, but I sure got airsick. Finally, I grabbed the stick and moved it back and forth. The plane was on a roller coaster ride.

"You want to land?"

"Please," I responded.

When we landed, I just lay down. I didn't feel very well. The pilot just looked at me and walked away with a big grin on his face. I decided right then: flying wasn't for me.

The next day, I was trucked away to Haleiwa Air Base, a small airstrip next to the ocean. I was assigned to a small three-man, cabin-like barracks tucked in among coconut palms. At night, we would hear the thud of coconuts hitting our roof. One of the occupants was named John Higgins, an alcoholic.

I introduced myself and flopped down on my bunk, took out my Bible, and started reading.

"So you're a Christian," John began. "I hope you don't believe that junk." He continued, "I can prove we all descended from monkeys and apes."

I didn't respond, and continued reading.

"Just feel at the base of your spine," he said, "and you'll feel a short bone where the tail used to be."

I looked up from my reading and quoted Genesis 1:1, "In the beginning God created the heavens and the earth," then continued reading.

John kept needling me, so I began quoting other scriptures. He just kept arguing. John was 39 years old, short, and very overweight. His nose was shiny red from all the booze he drank. He spent most of his time drunk. He hated the army and was soon to be discharged because the war in the Pacific was going so well that all men 39 and over would be released.

John's final words to me that last day: "You need to get together with Houchin and Duty; they both have your crazy ideas."

The next morning after breakfast, I went looking for the two. Ken Houchin worked in the clinic, and Ed Duty worked in the propeller shop. We soon became close friends and had Bible studies together.

Only God knows why I was assigned to a squadron that contained two strong Christians. We soon became known as the "Sky Pilots."

When I arrived at Haleiwa, we had a squadron of P-40's. I was assigned to the Operations Office. Sergeant Murphy was my boss. Besides a typewriter, calculator, and telephone, we had a teletype machine, the forerunner of the computer.

The squadron was divided into colors: Red, Blue, Green, and White. The pilots sat in the ready room awaiting a call from us. The radar station would call us at the Operations Office to send a squadron to check out anything suspicious that showed up on the radar screen. We would then relay the message to the pilots in the ready room.

GOD IS MY WITNESS   *11*

"Scramble Red Squadron to Angels 20." The sky was divided into quadrants so we and the pilots would know exactly where they were to look. Angels 20 meant they were to check out anything straight up at 20,000 feet. If there happened to be an enemy aircraft there, they were ordered to shoot it down.

After about two weeks, we were given the order to pack up everything. We were shipping out.

We were never told where we would be going, we just hurried to pack everything and waited.

We were sitting on our duffel bags when over the loud-speaker came the message, "Cancel the order to ship out; we're staying here." We weren't needed because the Marines, Army, and Navy were capturing island after island, getting closer and closer to Japan.

In the meantime, while we were waiting for new equipment, we were given two-day passes.

This happened on a Friday, so Saturday, Ken, Ed, and I went to Honolulu. Whenever we left the base, we had to carry a cumbersome gas mask, housed in a large bag with a shoulder strap. I have round shoulders, so the bag kept slipping off. I couldn't see why we needed to carry the gas mask—unless it was because of all the beans the mess hall served us. The Hawaiian Islands were so well secured (after the 1941 attack) that it would have been impossible for any enemy to attack us.

We wandered around Honolulu, went to the palace (Iolani Palace) of the island's kings, ate lunch at the YMCA, and returned to camp. Sunday morning we again hitchhiked to Honolulu so we could attend the Kaimuki Community Church, where we met a lot of the "Natives" and had a wonderful time.

Mr. and Mrs. Boone took us in like family. Mr. Boone served in the Army during WWI and was stationed on Oahu. He met his wife, who was of Japanese ancestry, married her, and remained in Honolulu. They had three boys. Their son Jim and I became good friends. Their son Stanley entered the Army as a pilot.

The congregation was made up of natives of Honolulu and a lot of servicemen of all branches. After each service, the ladies prepared meals for all of us, which gave us opportunity to meet the "Natives," Americans (from the mainland), Chinese, and—believe it or not—Japanese. They weren't all sent to camps in the U.S.

I was invited for Christmas dinner at a Japanese home. They ate with chopsticks—foreign to me. They did, however, come up with a knife, fork, and spoon just for me.

I was determined to learn to use chopsticks, so one day while on leave, I stopped in a Chinese restaurant.

I asked the Chinese waitress, "Can you teach me to eat with chopsticks?"

"Sure. What would you like to eat?"

"I don't have any idea, I've never eaten Chinese food before, and I have no idea what the menu says. What would you suggest?"

She came back with a huge plate of food and a pair of chopsticks for both of us. I was the only customer, so she helped me hold the chopsticks. I had an awful time trying

The force of the jolt was so severe that it drove one of the plane's machine guns six inches into solid rock. It took our medical doctor, and others, four hours to collect fifty pounds of his body.

"Why are you washing the body parts?" I asked the doctor.

"The Army requires that we collect all we can and wash every part before burial." The largest part was skin from his chest.

For a long time we were just jumping from one air base to another, so I went into the squadron commander's office and made a request.

"Since we don't seem to be getting into the war, would you consider my transferring to Headquarters at Hickam Field? The Army doesn't seem to be needing us because the Army and Marines are pushing the Japanese back to Tokyo. I would like to enter the University of Hawaii and pick up some college credits."

"I think I can arrange that for you." The next day, I was saying goodbye to all my friends. I was especially sad to leave Ken and Ed because we had become such good friends.

When I arrived at Hickam Field, I was assigned as messenger boy to carry messages to all the offices. One day, I delivered a confidential message to General Moore's office. He was not there, but his door was open. On the wall was a blown-up picture of Iwo Jima. Up till now, I had never heard of it.

# — 4 —

# *Off to War*

After duty that first day, I caught a bus for the U. of Hawaii and paid the $30 registration fee. I attended my first class the next day. That was my only class, because we were restricted to base. We were told we were heading for war, but we weren't told where. I now had confidential information I wasn't supposed to have.

We were on a roly-poly troop ship that constantly dipped and rolled, but I loved it. I especially enjoyed watching flying fish, as they jumped out of the water and flew for yards before diving back into the water, and the dolphins as they so gracefully swam alongside, as though protecting us.

The next program on our agenda: a severe tropical typhoon hit us. The little troop ship we were on was like a cork bobbing up and down and from side to side. I was on deck. At one point, I could almost touch the ocean, and the next swell, I could reach to the sky. Men were lined up along the rail feeding the fish. I loved it. I never did get seasick.

I spent most of my time deckside. Early one morning, I heard the roar of one of our sub chasers coming toward us. It stopped a few hundred yards in front of us and dropped depth charges. In minutes, I could see parts of a submarine floating to the surface: life vests, bits of clothing, and parts from the sub that would float. Scratch one submarine. However, there had been two Japanese submarines following us. Now they were down to only one, and that sub was sending messages from Tokyo Rose—for us.

"Why don't you do yourselves a favor, turn around and save your lives. You are not going to land on Iwo, you will be slaughtered..."

I did enjoy the classical music she played for us every night: Chopin, Mozart, and others. After getting us listening to classical music, she would periodically chime in with propaganda, and she had her facts pretty straight.

"Captain (name), your best friend was out with your wife last night. They were seen at a nice restaurant having a good time together. Poor you, out in this stormy weather going to your death."

After 28 days of zigzagging across the Pacific, we finally arrived at Iwo Jima, a small, narrow island approximately five miles long, but well-fortified. With one exception: water. Everything they did was by hand. For water, they used cement to make troughs around the many volcanic boulders. At the base, they planted 55-gallon drums to catch the rainwater. This was their water supply. By the time the Japanese surrendered, they were out of water. After we captured the island, our Navy Construction Battalion brought in drilling equipment, and we had lots of good, clean water.

We arrived at the south side of the island just before

dark, near the base of Mount Suribachi. We weren't sched-
uled to land until the next morning, so I went topside. As
I passed the galley, the cook stuck his head out the window
and asked, "Would you like a whole chicken?"

At a young age, I had a voracious appetite, so I
responded, "Sure."

I took the chicken to a steel spool on deck, sat down,
and watched the fireworks as I ate Army chicken. I hadn't
yet experienced the taste of war, so all the cannons firing,
the flash of red flames as the shells left the 80-mm guns
from the ships, and the fire from the flamethrowers burning out the caves that held the hidden Japanese soldiers
made me realize this was real. Before this, it was as though
I were watching a war movie.

That was soon to change. As I walked through a passage-
way on the way to disembark, a soldier came to me asking,
"Would you take this pencil and poke out my ear drum so
I can go on sick call?" He was so scared he was going to die
that he was searching for a way out. I told him "No!" and
kept on walking.

## — 5 —

# Landing on Iwo Jima

With full packs, we climbed over the rail and onto a rope ladder that fed into a landing craft. We were packed into that craft like sardines in a can. When we landed, the first thing I saw was an arm sticking up out of the sand. That was another inkling I had that this was war—it wasn't a game.

"Everybody pick a partner and dig yourselves a foxhole," the first Sergeant shouted. Everyone picked a foxhole partner except Buscus and me. Buscus was a short, skinny, egotistical Italian who knew everything about everything. Nobody liked him, which is why I ended up with him.

Because I held the rank of sergeant, I was given a detail to dig up the dead Japanese soldiers. We were to locate them, then pile the dead bodies alongside the road for a truck to pick up and take to a common grave.

We picked up several who had fallen on open ground. The stench of rotting flesh was so strong we had to wear gas masks. Then we came upon a Japanese body wedged in a deep hole between two huge boulders.

I made a loop in a rope. As we lowered the rope onto the man's head and tried to pull him up, his head came off.

He still had his battle helmet on, so I rolled his head to one side and left to get a grappling hook. I was walking back when I met a Marine who had just landed.

"Dddddid you sssee thhhhhthat helmet with a head in it?" he asked in complete bewilderment. He was visibly frightened by what he had just witnessed.

"Yeah, I just put it there," I commented. He walked away, shaking his head. He, too, had just realized he was in a real war.

War does strange things to one's mind. After a few days of digging up the dead, they no longer looked human. They became nothing more than digging up dead wood. A young soldier came to me and asked, "How much gold do you have?"

"I don't have any gold, why do you ask?" He then reached into his pocket and pulled out a handful of gold fillings.

"Where did you get those?" I asked, knowing full well what he had done.

"I figured the dead didn't need their fillings anymore, so I kicked out their teeth for the fillings." That almost made me sick to think we had stooped to that low. I didn't even answer the kid, so he just calmly walked away.

It was dark when Buscus and I crawled into our foxhole and pulled the tarp over us. We were almost asleep when we heard the sound of gunfire. As I looked up, I could see a small hole in our tarp. A Japanese soldier out looking for water had spotted the tarp covering our foxhole, assumed there was only one person, and shot one shot in the middle. The bullet landed between our elbows, missing us by less than an inch. We didn't make a move. It would have been normal for him to have fired three bullets, which would have hit one or both of us. Why he shot only one bullet was only God's hand protecting us. Psalms 32:8 says, "I will watch over you and be your advisor" (The Jerusalem Bible). I kept the spent bullet for a long time but finally lost it during one of our many moves.

The island was finally pretty secure, and the Navy Construction Battalion had built showers for us next to the overhanging cliff that overlooked the ocean. One evening, the USO was holding a program for the men, complete with scantily clad girls. I decided I didn't want to attend. By this time, we were out of foxholes and into four-man tents. I decided to take a shower.

As I stepped out of the shower, I was making my way back to my tent. The night was pitch black. As I was stumbling in the dark, a Japanese soldier came up behind me and jumped on my back to take me down and either choke me or stab me. But I was stronger than he, so I reached back, grabbed him by his head, and slammed him onto the ground. He quickly got up and ran away. I wish I had held him on the ground so I could have carried him back to camp, but it happened so fast, I didn't have time to think. I didn't tell anyone because I didn't think they would have believed me, anyway.

From here on out, life was pretty much routine. The Construction Battalion had constructed several metal buildings for Seventh Fighter Command offices. I was assigned to work in one of the offices. However, a Warrant

Officer didn't like Christians. He harassed me all day long. Matthew 5:11 says, "Blessed are you when men cast insults at you and persecute you and say all kinds of evil against you falsely on account of Me, rejoice and be glad..." That's a hard pill to swallow when one is going through the harassment.

After I had put up with the harassment several days, the Adjutant of the Fifteenth Fighter Wing saw my problem and asked if I would like to work for him as his private secretary. He said he needed someone to write letters to the families of those who were killed. I was an excellent typist, so I jumped at the chance. Not only did I have my own desk in his office but I had access to his jeep, which I could use anytime I was off duty. All I really had to do was keep track of the money the soldiers deposited in the safe and write letters to the families of the solders who had been killed. One woman wrote about her husband who was listed as having been killed. She couldn't accept his death as real, so she wrote asking Captain Wolten if he would take a picture of her husband's grave marker.

I was handed the letter and asked to find his grave marker and send the woman a letter enclosing a picture. I guess the letter I wrote was what he wanted because he signed the letter. I really hurt for that wife, whose husband had given the ultimate sacrifice.

There were still a few Japanese holdouts hidden back in the caves because they kept conducting small sporadic banzai raids. We were so heavily guarded they couldn't do us any damage.

However, we still had to pull guard duty. My name came up for guard post number two. The first sergeant did something I had never known him to do—he scratched my name and inserted another. Our area was still surrounded by a single wire hooked to flares.

Around 11 p.m. that same night, a young Japanese soldier came out of a cave, looking for water, and tripped the flare. The entire area lit up like Christmas. The two on guard duty had no choice but to shoot him. He looked to be about 12 years of age. If my name had not been changed, I would have had no choice but to shoot the little boy. I wasn't mad at anyone; I didn't want to kill anybody, not even the Japanese, but I would not have had a choice—I would have had to shoot him.

A young man from Coral Gables, Florida, moved into our tent. His name was Conrad Thompson, known as Connie. He and I became very close friends. Connie had the type of personality that could talk anyone out of anything.

One day I suggested, "If we could come up with a two-man tent, we could put it up overlooking the ocean." Connie didn't make any comment, but the next day he came in dragging a two-man tent.

"Where'd you say you wanted to put it?" We found a good spot on the edge of the cliff overlooking the ocean.

"What else do we need?"

"We need a few two-by-fours, a handsaw, hammer, and assortment of nails."

Sure enough, he came back with several two-by-fours of various lengths, a handsaw, hammer, and nails.

"Where are you getting all this stuff?"

"Don't ask," was all he would say.

I set to work constructing a floor about twelve inches from the ground, walls up about four feet high, with an opening for the door. When it was completed, the two of us fitted the tent over the framework and—presto!—we had our own little home away from home. I made steps into the tent and a bunk for each of us, with a writing desk between. I made a drawer that fit under our bunks to store our gear. One day when we were lying on our bunks, I commented to Connie, "It would be real nice if we had a radio." The Service Organization had just installed a radio station on the island.

The next day, Connie came in with a radio.

"Where'dja get that?" I asked.

"I traded my wristwatch for it" was his nonchalant answer.

Another night, we were lying on our bunks when I suggested, "You know, if we had an empty wing tank, by using the hot sun, we could make our own hot shower. We could pipe the rainwater into the tank from the roof, and with the sun heating up the water, we could have our own shower."

The very next day, Connie came in dragging a wing tank. "What else do we need?"

"We need some plumbing: a short pipe and a shut-off valve. I never did find out where he scrounged all this material, but I built a stand for the wing tank and put in the plumbing, and we had our own hot water shower.

One Sunday afternoon, I was sitting on the step, watching a boy pounding something on the edge of a box, when I heard an explosion. He had been trying to unscrew a detonator from a large shell. When it exploded, it took off his fingers and peppered his body with shell fragments.

The commanding officer was furious. He wanted to court-martial the boy, but the medical doctor said, "We are in a war zone. Even though the boy did something stupid, I am going to list it as injured on a battlefield."

Another day, I was sitting on the step to our tent, enjoying the sunshine. I was watching men rolling empty gasoline barrels down the slope to load onto a waiting ship. One of the men rolled a barrel over a land mine, and I heard the explosion. The mine blew off both of his legs. "I won't be able to play ball! I won't be able to play ball," he screamed. In civilian life, he must have been a professional ball player.

The weather was warm and beautiful. I could see storm clouds forming, and before long, we were hit with another typhoon. All the standing tents were blown to the ground—except our little two-man tent. It stood the storm.

Connie's and my next job was helping put the tents back up so the men would have a place to sleep.

The war was almost over. However, there were a few banzai die-hards still hiding in the caves and coming out at night to shoot as many Americans as they could. We were so well secured, the Japanese were the ones killed. We knew there were dead Japanese soldiers, but in the morning we couldn't find anyone. We soon learned that before daylight, they would haul the dead back into the caves.

Being a young, foolish soldier, I would take a flashlight and go into the caves to explore, walking over dead bodies piled two and three deep. They didn't rot because of the extremely dry caves—they mummified.

The caves meandered in long tunnels, occasionally branching off in side caves. After I emerged from one of the caves, seventeen Japanese soldiers came out to surrender. If they had seen me, a crazy kid walking along with just a flashlight, they must have thought the war was over and decided to come out. Being without food or water probably had something to do with their decision.

April 12, I was standing in line for lunch when the loudspeaker announced: "Now hear this: President Roosevelt passed away today. Harry Truman has been sworn in as our new president." President Roosevelt did not live to see World War II come to an end. April 12, 1945, he died of a brain hemorrhage.

President Truman ordered the use of atomic bombs on Japan, and Japan surrendered September 9. We were finally going home. I had served my country for a little over three years.

We were chosen to leave Iwo Jima based on our time on the island. While we awaited our orders, there wasn't anything for us to do but sit and wait. A few days later, my orders came. I said goodbye to Connie and friends, then entered a landing craft, and was ferried out to a destroyer. It was a beautiful, warm day. I was standing on the prow of that huge ship as it plowed along, water sprays washing my face. I would soon be a civilian again. I watched as Iwo Jima slowly faded in the distance. A new chapter was about to unfold in my life. Whom would I marry? What would I do? What did God have in store for me? I didn't know it then, but I was to find out—God already had my life planned out.

# COMING HOME

## – 6 –

## From Soldier to Civilian

The same day I left Iwo Jima for my trip back home, we arrived at the island of Saipan. We were told we would be in Saipan for several days while the Army was scheduling our departure.

I had learned about "suicide cliff," where the Japanese officers ordered the civilians to jump to their deaths. There were a number of Japanese civilians—older men, women, and children—living on the island when the Japanese soldiers knew they had lost the island, so they ordered all the civilians to jump to their deaths. The cliff, overlooking the ocean, was approximately 300 feet to the bottom. They were told that if they were captured by the Americans, they would be raped and killed. Those who refused to jump were pushed.

As soon as we arrived at Saipan, I ditched my duffel bag and headed for the opposite side of the island. I hadn't walked very far when I was picked up by an Army truck and driven to the cliff.

As I stood on the cliff edge, I could picture in my mind the awful tragedy. I could envision the old men, women, and children jumping to their deaths on the rocks below.

It was a long drop. Hebrews 9:27 came to my mind: "And inasmuch as it is appointed for men to die once, and after this comes the judgment." How sad.

When I arrived back at the makeshift camp, I was told my name was posted to draw kitchen patrol (KP). I ignored the list, and the next day I was again on another roly-poly troop ship. It took us 28 days to get to Iwo Jima, but it took only 14 days before I passed under the same Golden Gate Bridge I passed under on my way out.

As soon as we landed on U.S. soil, three of us took a taxi to the finest restaurant the driver suggested. We all had T-bone steaks with everything that could be put on the plate.

Later that same day, I was on a train headed for Seattle. Two days later, I was on a bus to Fort Lewis, where my long journey began.

I spent the night at Fort Lewis and the next morning was assigned an Army counselor, who brought us up to date on new laws concerning veterans. He told us that President Truman had signed an order giving certain rights to veterans including college and university tuition, the full four years paid for by the government.

I could have gone back to my old job with the Army Engineers. When I enlisted, I was told my job would be waiting for me if I wanted it back. I thought about it for a while, but decided it didn't pay more than enough for my own needs, let alone those of a family, should I decide to marry.

After weighing my options, I finally decided to check out Seattle Pacific College. After talking to a counselor, I decided to enroll.

I sent in my transcript from my high school and was accepted. At that time, Seattle Pacific was a rather small college. The Veteran's Administration paid for everything, including books and my room and board. A great deal, plus a monthly stipend.

I met the girl of my dreams at the college cafeteria the day I entered SPC. I introduced myself and met a young woman from Texas named Ruth Smith. I saw her occasionally on campus, but I didn't pay a whole lot of attention to her. There were lots of girls attending Seattle Pacific.

A pianist was holding a recital at the college church across the street. We were asked to hand out fliers advertising the concert. I signed up and was assigned to a group to go door-to-door, handing out flyers.

That same day, I received a note in my mailbox stating, "It's OK by me," signed with a capital "R." I roomed with two other young men. I went to the room and asked, "Who put this note in my mailbox?" They both denied putting it in my box. One of the men looked at the note and said, "That's a girl's handwriting."

The only girl I knew on campus was Ruth Smith, but I couldn't just go up to her and ask, "Did you put a note in my box?"

I was assigned a different group than Ruth to hand out flyers, but during the evening, I worked my way to her group. After handing out flyers, we were invited to the Fellowship Hall in the basement of the church for coffee and donuts.

At a break in our walk around the neighborhood, I went up to Ruth, and in the course of our conversation, I asked casually, "By the way, I received a note in my box today with the initial 'R.' The note said, 'It's OK by me.' Did you put a note in my box?"

She answered, "Did you put a note in my box asking for a date to the concert?"

I knew if I said, "No," she would probably have denied putting the note in my box. I said, "Yes, I did."

Then she admitted putting the note in my box.

I responded, "I didn't put the note in your box."

She then tried to deny, half-heartedly, putting the note in my box, but I did get the feeling she just didn't want to admit to putting it there.

As we entered the church basement, there was a notepad asking those who wanted to attend the concert to please sign. I said, "If you are planning to attend the concert, why don't you sign first?" As she signed, I took out the note and compared the two R's.

I smiled at her as I compared the two R's. "OK, I did write the note," she admitted.

"What did the note say?" was my next question.

"The note asked me for date to this concert," she replied.

"If somebody wants us to get together, would you consider going to the concert with me?" We never did find out who wrote the note.

This happened in May or June of my first year at Seattle Pacific. We were married December 22 of that same year—64 years ago.

*The newlyweds.*

# — 7 —

# Buying a House

During my time in the Army, I didn't spend money for things I didn't need, but I saved every penny I could. When I left the Army, I had over a thousand dollars in my bank account. I looked around for a house I could afford. Two blocks from the college, I saw a sign on a three-story house, "For Sale."

I took down the phone number and called the realtor. "I have the house listed at $6,000," he responded.

"How much is the down payment?"

"For $600, you can move in."

From what I had saved from my time in the Army, I paid the man the $600. I now owned a house. I didn't know anything about houses. I looked at the roof and siding, and they both looked OK.

I showed Ruth the house, and we moved in December 23—no furniture, no pots and pans, no dishes—no nothing. We were just two newlyweds still in college.

I drew more money from my bank so we could purchase a bedroom set, a dining room table and chairs, and for ten dollars, an old worn-out couch. Ruth was an expert seamstress. She purchased materials to cover the couch and made the couch look new. Little by little, we were able to get the things we needed to set up housekeeping.

I have already said, I didn't know anything about houses—I didn't. As one ran upstairs, the whole house shook like we were in an earthquake. The house didn't have a solid foundation. It was built on wood blocks set in the ground which had long ago rotted. The house was sitting on a dirt foundation. No wonder it shook when we ran upstairs. We lived in that shaky house for more than a year.

*The Queen Anne triplex*
*BEFORE Bob added a foundation.*

Ruth graduated and obtained a job as a secretary for Anderson Buick Co. She was cooped up in a very small office with a boss who lit one cigarette after another, leaving the butt to smolder. She had constant headaches.

While we were dating, we learned we each had a desire to serve the Lord, possibly as missionaries. We talked with one of the professors, who, during WWII, had worked for the U. S. Government in Peru, South America, harvesting the millions of fish that inhabited the Guano Islands off Lima. The fish became fat from the droppings from the millions of Guano birds that made their nests on the island. The U.S. Government wanted the processed fish to help feed our troops.

Dr. McMillan introduced Ruth and me to Wycliffe Bible Translators. While in Peru, he was impressed with their work among various tribes who did not have the Bible in their native languages. He gave us the address to the Wycliffe office.

– 8 –

## Learning Construction Skills

Ruth and I attended a small church in West Seattle. One of the attendees claimed he was a building contractor. I had no reason to doubt him, so one Sunday, I asked him to stop by our house and give me an estimate what it would cost to build a concrete foundation.

After my last class the next day, I went home to find the east end of the daylight basement gutted. The house was standing on two-by-fours. The "contractor" was nowhere—he had gone home.

"Now what do I do?" I called Ruth at work, and she gave me the pastor's telephone number, who gave me the "contractor's" number. I called him and said, "I only asked you for an estimate."

"I thought you wanted me to put a new foundation under your house," he commented.

"I only wanted you to give me an estimate. Now that the basement is all torn out, what materials do you need to finish the job? And how much will you charge for your work?" His amount seemed reasonable.

"What do I need to order for you to start?" He gave me a list of the number of concrete blocks and the amount of sand needed. I didn't know where I would get the money, but I ordered the materials.

My father's brother lived in South Seattle, so I called him to ask if he would lend me $1,500. He said he would, so I borrowed the money from him.

When Ruth and I married, we agreed we would not go into debt, that we would only spend money we had at the time. That worked just fine until the "house problem" came up.

The "problem" was thrown at us; it wasn't planned. We were forced into it. How did this fit into God's plan for us?

We believed "that God causes all things to work together for good to those who love God, to those who are called according to His purpose" (Romans 8:28). How in the world was this going to work for good? It didn't make sense to us.

The materials were delivered so the contractor could start work. I called, and the next day he was ready to begin the foundation.

Ruth went to work, and I went to my classes. After class that evening, I returned to the house to find concrete blocks set up under the wall. There was a problem. He didn't use a plumb to check the location of the blocks to the wall. Four inches of the wall would sit on the blocks, but four inches would be outside the wall. I took one look at the blocks, drove to the hardware store, and purchased a sledge hammer. I knocked out the blocks and called the "contractor" to tell him I didn't want him back. I explained the problem to him. He never returned.

The next Sunday, I talked to the pastor about the problem. His comment was, "Didn't you know he was mentally ill?"

"You knew I hired him to work on my house?" I asked.

"I thought you knew he was a mental case."

We didn't, and no one had told us.

My next question was, "What do I do now?"

I didn't know anything about working with concrete, so I went to the library and found a book on working with concrete and foundations.

I made a wooden box eight inches high, five feet long, and three feet wide for mixing the sand, cement, and water to make the concrete.

I don't know what I did with the concrete blocks. I probably gave them away to get rid of them. I don't remember. I just wanted them out of my way.

My next project: dig a trench three feet deep and ten inches wide around the end of the house so I could build the forms, into which I could pour the concrete mix. I needed to pour a ten-inch-wide footing and three-foot-high form eight inches wide on which to build the foundation wall.

I also purchased rebar—steel bars to tie the foundation together. In four-foot sections, I hand-mixed the concrete and poured short sections of the foundation.

I purchased a hydraulic truck jack with which I jacked up sections of the wall before I poured the concrete. And after placing a two-by-six plank on the mixed concrete when the concrete was set, I could lower the wall onto the plate and move on to the next four-foot section. I did this slowly all the way around the house—mixing all the concrete by hand. When it was completed, the house sat on a solid foundation, and the building no longer shook as we walked upstairs. I was now a professional foundation builder.

When Ruth came home from work, we both stood and admired my work. Then one of us said, looking at the daylight basement, "Why don't we make an apartment in the basement that we could rent out?"

"Since I have to rebuild the wall anyway, I might as well refurbish the entire basement and build a wall at the far end to enclose a bedroom. There is already a bathroom with a shower, and the room next to it could be used as a kitchen. That still leaves a good-sized living room."

The two of us worked late nights making the basement into an apartment. In the process, I learned to do electrical wiring, plumbing, and plasterboarding, including the taping. We also installed a large gas heater.

At Seattle Pacific, I enrolled in a cabinetmaking class. The government paid for all the materials, so I made kitchen cabinets for our house. I made all the upper cabinets for our kitchen.

Our next project was our living quarters in the center of the house. One of my classmates' fathers had equipment for finishing oak floors. Half of our dining room didn't have oak. My brother's father-in-law installed oak floors. My brother talked him into finishing the floor with oak. He only charged for the oak. My classmate's father finished the floor. It turned out beautifully.

"Now that we are getting the house in good shape, why don't I check with the city to see if we could make part of the upstairs into a small apartment?"

That sounded like a good idea to Ruth, so I went to the City Building Department.

"The first thing you have to do is get your neighbors' OK."

The gentleman was very helpful and gave me a printed contract that I could take around to my neighbors. They all signed it, giving me permission to build the apartment.

We had to submit a drawing of our plans, which we did, and it was approved by the city. Back then, a permit only cost five dollars. Try that today!

Ruth didn't have any idea what she was getting into when she said "Yes." That was 64 years ago.

We were now the proud owners of a triplex. Only one problem: although we vowed when we got married we would not go into debt, that we would live on whatever money we earned, that "vow" went down the drain when we asked the contractor to give me an estimate of what a foundation would cost.

We lived so frugally, instead buying expensive beef, we bought horse meat from a butcher shop on Greenwood Avenue that sold horse meat.

I stopped by and bought a nice roast. Ruth cooked it like she would a beef roast, but it was so dry we couldn't eat it. Horse meat doesn't have veins of fat like beef.

Besides, every time I took a bite of the roast I could see old Nelly (the horse I rode as a child) grazing on the field.

A few days later, I came home with some steaks. "If we're planning on going as missionaries, we might as well get used to eating horse meat," I suggested.

This time Ruth made Swiss steaks, and they were delicious. She learned that horse meat has to be cooked with moist heat. From then on, we had lots of Swiss steaks.

One Sunday afternoon, we invited a professor and his wife to have lunch with us. After the meal, the wife wanted to help with dishes. As she looked at the pan with all that meat, she commented, "My, you cooked a lot of meat!" We wouldn't have dared tell her it was horse meat. I'm not sure she would have enjoyed the meat quite so much as she claimed during lunch.

Ruth commented rather casually, "I work every day, so to make meal planning easier, I do most of the cooking on weekends," which she did.

The wife's response was, "So do I."

Stan and Ann Boone, classmates who were at Seattle Pacific the same time we were, had to move out of their house. They were busy packing, so Ruth called and said we would bring supper so they could keep packing.

Finishing a nice meal (including horse Swiss steaks), Stan was standing in the kitchen, munching on another steak.

I asked, "Have you ever eaten horse meat?"

"Not that I know of."

"You are eating a steak right now."

"I am? Well, it sure tastes good."

This is the same Stanley Boone I met in Hawaii, the son of the Boones who were so nice to me.

By this time, we were almost finished with our building project. One hurdle stood in our way. We had spent all the money my uncle loaned us, and we were broke. That didn't matter to the stores from which I purchased the building materials. They kept sending collection letters.

"Lord, what do we do now—how are we going to pay our creditors?"

Our neighbor lady, who lost her bomber-pilot husband (he was shot down over Germany), asked if we would like to accompany her to Canada to visit a couple of college friends who were pastors of a small church.

"It won't cost you anything; I just don't want to drive there by myself, and I'd appreciate your going with me."

We thought we were going to lose the house anyway, so we decided to take the time off. We had worked every day, six days a week, late into the night. We were tired and needed a rest.

We did go with Winnie and had a wonderful, restful time. We did not know the State of Washington had voted to give everyone who had served in the military during WWII a bonus of $500. When we arrived home and checked our mail, there was a check for the amount of $500, enough money to pay off our debts and enough to complete the house.

We had tried to refinance the house, but because it wasn't completed, the loan company turned us down. We resubmitted the application, and thanks to an executive who had graduated from Seattle Pacific, we were given a new loan. We were now able to pay back the money my uncle had loaned us. The monthly mortgage was still under $100, including the property tax.

We had applied to Wycliffe Bible Translators to become members. However, before we were given final approval, we had to pass "Jungle Training."

OFF TO MEXICO

– 9 –

# Jungle Training

We had to travel to southern Mexico, to the state of Chiapas, to a very remote part of the state—no roads, no telephone, no nothing. We were flown in by a small plane and left to survive with about 25 others.

*Ruth and Bob at jungle camp: Ruth caught all but one of the fish this day at Jungle Training.*

The purpose was to see how we could adapt to very primitive living conditions. The main base had houses, such as they were. But after a short time, we had to move into the jungle area and build our own lean-to shelters out of jungle materials. Ruth and I built our own "home," including a fire table on which to cook our meals. Many had brought along air mattresses. We were so poor, we didn't have money to buy one. We made a makeshift bed of poles and covered it with leaves. In the night, the leaves would bunch up in clumps—not very comfortable.

We completed the roof, and it looked pretty good. During a heavy rainstorm, Ruth kept saying she was getting wet. The next morning, Ruth and her blankets were all wet. The roof leaked over her side of the bed. My side was nice and dry.

After three months, we were flown out to Tuxtla, where we had stored our car.

Before we left for jungle camp, we had saved all the money we could. And after checking maps, we figured we had just enough money to get to Tuxtla and back. We could eat one good meal a day, and the rest of the time we lived on bread, milk, and sandwich meats. When we could, we would stop by relatives and friends along the way, which weren't many. The rest of the time, we slept in the car.

Before we left Tuxtla, we counted our money, and we still had enough to get us home.

Herb and Grace Fuqua and a nurse left the base by the small plane ahead of us, so they were well on their way by the time we got to Tuxtla. We left and had traveled several miles, crossing the mountains, when we spotted the Fuquas by the side of the road. We asked if everything was OK.

"We have a problem with the car: it started to make real loud noises. We stopped at several garages along the way, but they didn't know what was wrong."

"Let me look at it." Because of the ages of the cars I owned, I always carried my tools with me. I had them in the trunk this time, too.

I pulled each spark plug. On the number two piston, there wasn't any compression.

"You have a broken piston." Herb didn't know anything about mechanics, so I said, "We'll stay here with you, and in the morning, let's take the motor apart and see what we can do to fix the problem."

During the night I came down with Montezuma's revenge. I was very sick with a bad case of diarrhea. I spent the night running to the bushes. The nurse, Amy, took over my care.

The next morning, I lay on a borrowed air mattress, instructing Herb how to take the engine apart, piece by piece. Fortunately, I had enough tools to completely rebuild an engine. When Herb pulled the piston, it was badly shattered.

The nearest town was fifty miles away. "Take our car and go to town. They just might have a piston for your car." About two hours later Herb came with a new piston, rings, and a connecting rod.

In reverse order, I directed Herb in putting all the parts back together. When it was completed, the car purred like new.

God had fulfilled Matthew 6:8, "...your father knows what you need, before you ask Him." God was looking out for the Fuquas, just as He was for us.

*Bob and Ruth work on a project during Jungle Training.*

— 10 —

## Hospitalized in Mexico

We were just about to leave when a car with two Americans drove up.

"You people look like missionaries." When we came out of jungle training, our clothes were all stained with banana juice and from cooking on open fires. We looked like we had been living in primitive conditions—we needed to find a laundry.

"We need to get Bob to a hospital," Amy commented.

"We live in Puebla, which has a hospital. You are welcome to stay with us. We have a large home, but not much furniture, so if you don't mind sleeping on the floor, you are welcome. The hospital is not far from our home."

Ruth drove me to the hospital. After three days, I was released. But when I paid the hospital bill, there wasn't enough money left for us to get home.

We prayed the prayer that we've prayed so many times in our married life—"Lord, what do we do now?"

We weren't planning on stopping in Mexico City but had planned to travel on. Now, we didn't have a choice.

We did stop at the Wycliffe house, where we were allowed to stay three days. There was a limit of three days because there were so many stopping there to spend the night that they had to put a limit on the time we could stay there.

No one knew we were stopping in Mexico City. We didn't even know. In fact, we didn't write any letters while in Mexico. We never told anyone about our financial problem. We only prayed, "Lord, what do we do now?"

The morning we were supposed to leave, we were sitting at breakfast. The director came over to our table and handed me a letter. To our complete amazement, it was Ruth's Income Tax refund, and there was enough money to pay our room and board and make it back home.

There is only one explanation—Matthew 6. I estimated the letter would have taken approximately five days to arrive in Mexico City. We didn't know we would be in Mexico City, but God did.

There are several more instances in our married life where an unseen hand worked miracles, but I will mention only a few more.

ON TO PERU

– 11 –

## Preparing for Peru

We were accepted by Wycliffe, but there was one obstacle: we had to raise our own support. I have never begged for anything in my life, and for me to ask churches, and individuals, to support us was not in my nature. I am not a good public speaker, and for me to stand before an audience and ask for money to pay our way to Peru and to pledge money for our support was not, as one would say, "my cup of tea."

I did speak at a few churches, but the results were minimal at best. Ruth and I talked about selling the house we had worked so hard to make into a triplex.

We prayed about it and finally decided, if God wanted us to serve Him as missionaries in Peru, we would put the house up for sale. That was a hard choice. We let the earnest money lapse three times before we finally signed. We read in Luke 12:15, "...a man's life is not made secure by what he owns" (The Jerusalem Bible).

As a young man, I decided that those whose funerals I attended did not take anything with them as they left this world. All they worked for, they left behind. I decided then I would not work for "things," that I wanted my life to account for something. I never have wanted to be wealthy.

When the paperwork was finally completed, we ended up with $5,000 that we could use. That was a lot of money at that time—1953.

We began packing. I had worked on automobiles since I was 12 years old. I bought my first car when I was 12 years old—a Star. I paid five dollars for it. Most people have never heard of a car called Star. It wasn't very good, so the company did not survive. But I learned to take it apart and put it back together. I drove it until I bought a Model T Ford—for five dollars. In the early 1940s, we did not have to have a driver's license. Anyway, I was only 12 years old.

Johnny Hillstrom, Avon Miller, and I each bought ourselves Model T's. We had a lot of fun racing each other on a long, straight length of road near our homes. However, I could beat them because my Ford had a Browney transmission. As we raced along, I could engage the Browney and leave them in the dust.

As Ruth and I were packing for Peru, I had enough tools to rebuild an engine. And having learned construction while rebuilding our house, I had a lot of carpentry tools.

"What should I do with these tools?" I asked Ruth. She didn't respond. "Since they are paid for, I might as well take them along."

"What would I do with mechanic's tools in the jungle of Peru?" was my next question. I didn't know it at the time, but God knew. I also had a blowtorch, a soldering iron, solder, and flux left over from working on the house.

"Should I take these along? What would I need them for in Peru?" I didn't know, but God did.

To this day, I don't understand why I packed those heavy items to take along to work in a primitive tribal location where the Indians' material possessions were paddles, canoes, a few pieces of clothing, machetes, and maybe a pot or two.

## — 12 —

# Gaining an Entrance to the Orejon Tribe

The Indian tribes of Peru were governed by a "Patron" system. These Patrons were supposed to take care of the Indian tribes. However, they usually exploited the Indians. That was the case among the Orejons we were trying to reach. Mrs. Rios lived at the mouth of the Sucusari River—a small river that empties into the Napo River, that flows into the Amazon just below the interior city of Iquitos.

We were told we had to get her permission to enter the tribe. She gave us permission to store our boxes and barrels under her house. At the beginning she seemed very cordial, but she warned us that it would be difficult to work among the Orejons because she often sent them away from the village to work for her. We finally got her OK to have a small house built a short distance up the Sucusari River, where we had a small grass-roofed house built for us. As the Indians brought goods to her house for her to sell, they would stop by our house. We would give them such items as fishhooks, cloth, and other small items they could use.

*Building their house in the Peruvian jungle.*

One day a Peruvian walked up the forty-some steps from the river to our house. As was usual with the Peruvians who lived along the banks of the Napo, they would begin with small talk, or bring us a gift of eggs.

Finally, I would ask, "What can I do for you?" I always knew they wanted something.

"My name is Señor Godoy. I am the Patron of the Arabela Indians who live up the Curaray River. My outboard motor broke down at the mouth of your river. I heard you can repair motors."

I had gained quite a reputation for my mechanical skills among those living on the Napo. I was called upon frequently to repair their outboard motors.

"If you can bring your outboard to my house, I will see if I can repair it."

One of his peons, a workman, lugged the heavy outboard and placed it next to our house.

Now I knew why God (that's the only explanation I have) "made" me bring along my tools. I removed the flywheel and could see a loose wire that was hooked to the condenser. Now I knew why I had the soldering iron, solder, and flux. I lit the torch and soldered the wire back onto the condenser.

We invited Mr. Godoy to have dinner with us. In the course of the evening, he asked, "Why did the two of you leave your beautiful homes in the States to come down here to live like this?"

Mr. Godoy was from Lima. In fact, he had a wife and family in Lima, but he was in the jungle because he made his living here.

We explained why we were here, that this was where God had directed us to live and that we were here to learn the Orejon language and translate the Bible into their language.

His next question: "Are their others in your group that could do this for the Arabelas?" We knew the Arabelas were located somewhere in the north part of Peru, but we didn't know where.

The next morning we cranked up our generator, called the base at Yarina Cocha, talked with our director, Cameron Townsend, and told him.

"A young couple just arrived at Yarina Cocha and were looking for a place to serve. Their names are Roland and Furne Rich," Uncle Cam told us.

Uncle Cam (as he was always referred to) talked with Roland and Furne about the Arabela Tribe. They thought about it, prayed about their working among the Arabelas, and decided they would like to work among the Arabelas.

The next day, they were flown to our place on the Sucusari River. A day or two later, Roland and I flagged down a riverboat going up the Napo. The boat was taking supplies to the army base at the mouth of the Curaray River.

The Arabelas live on the upper reaches of the Curaray river. I don't know if they live in Peru or Ecuador. Roland and Furne returned to Yarina Cocha to make preparations to work among the Arabelas.

Today the Arabelas have the Word of God in their native language, a church, and a school.

Although Roland and Furne no longer live among the Arabelas, they now live in California, and keep in touch with the leaders of the Arabelas by our modern technology, the cell phone.

Why did my cousin give me a pair of forceps? I don't know why I had them with me at this particular time. Enrique, a Peruvian living on the Napo, paddled to our house one day. After a lot of small talk, he said, "My daughter is very sick, could you cure her?" They always wanted me to cure their ailments.

I responded, "Let's go to your house so I can look at her to see if I can do anything for her."

I started my outboard, and we went to Enrique's. As I stepped into their grass shack, Olefina was sitting on a chair with a dirty rag wrapped around her jaw.

I had her open her mouth, and I could see a very badly inflamed tooth.

"Enrique, her tooth has to come out. I have a pair of forceps, but I don't have any Novocain to deaden her jaw."

"Do what you have to do. She is so sick she can't even walk."

I asked Olefina if she wanted me to remove her tooth, she responded in Spanish, "Please."

I took out the forceps, held her head in the crook of my arm, and began twisting and pulling on the tooth. The day was hot. We were both perspiring profusely. I twisted and pulled as long as she could stand the pain, then we would rest. After an hour, the tooth finally came out.

I put a cotton swab to stop the bleeding, gave her a shot of antibiotics, and left. A week later, I stopped by to see how she was doing. She was down at the river, washing clothes.

For my service, Enrique gave me a hen we named "Blondy." It was the best laying hen we ever had. Most hens will lay a dozen eggs, then want to sit. Blondy just kept on laying eggs. She didn't seem to ever want to sit on her eggs.

Up until now, I didn't know why my doctor cousin insisted I take the forceps to Peru—now I knew. Matthew 6:9 says, "Before you ask God, He knows what you need." And Proverbs 3:5-6 says, "Trust wholeheartedly in Yahweh, put no faith in your own perception; in every course you take, have Him in mind: He will see that your paths are smooth"(The Jerusalem Bible). If we could only keep this in mind, our lives would be less stressful.

Contrary to the wishes of the Señora, I would make periodic trips to the village way up the Sucusari River. On one trip, the Matriarchal Mother of the tribe was very ill. I took her temperature, and it was 105. I left her, returned home, and called our doctor on our radio. He said there was very little chance she would survive. The culture of the tribe was such that if the Matriarchal Mother died, the entire tribe would scatter, and it would have been very difficult to reach them.

Ruth and I prayed and asked God to spare her life. Early the next morning, I returned to the village with my medical kit. Maria was at the point of death. I gave her a shot of antibiotics, left sulfa pills for her husband to give her, and left for home.

The water in the river was still high enough, so the next day, I returned to see her sitting on a chair—her fever was down. She recovered completely.

Her husband asked me, "Why did you come to cure Maria when the Señora never would?"

As best as I could, I tried to explain to him our mission. I had only learned a few expressions in his language, but with my limited Spanish, I tried. When Miguel was a young man, he was captured by a renegade Peruvian general who tried to take over the eastern part of Peru. His coup failed, and Miguel was able to return to his village, but he had learned a lot of Spanish.

*Leon, an Orejon man, allows us to photograph his fine example of the huge ear disks they wore.*

— 13 —

# The Sewing Machine

The clothing they had was made by the Señora, Mrs. Rios. They were poorly made but did cover their bodies. We had written to our church in Seattle and told them we needed a treadle sewing machine so Ruth could teach the women to sew. A member of the church wrote and said he was sending us two sewing machines.

On one of our many long trips down the Napo and up the Sucusari, we had mentioned to Miguel (Maria's husband) that we would like to live in the village so Ruth could teach the women to sew.

When Miguel realized we were there to help them and not hurt them, he asked, "When are you going to teach the women to sew?"

My answer was, "As soon as you build us a house, we will come."

"We will build you a house right away."

We then prepared to move into the village. At first, we moved into one end of their 80-foot-long house and set up camping. It wasn't very secure, and it was open to their curiosity.

When our little grass shack was completed, we moved

and had our own privacy—for the most part. However, they had constructed a small porch on the south end of our house. That was the perfect place for the entire tribe to gather. It was wonderful for learning their language but not very good for our privacy.

I don't know how Ruth kept her sanity the way we were moving about, having to scrounge through boxes and barrels to find what she needed just to take care of our basic needs. But she hung in there like a trooper.

When our house was completed, we were told over the radio that our two sewing machines had arrived.

Another of God's provisions: When we were living in the village, often the Sucusari was so low in water Miguel told us, "You are our prisoners now. There isn't enough water for you to leave."

*Bob with an Orejon boy, Miguel, and Mateo.*

It would have been impossible for us to walk out because of the many swamps between us and the Napo River.

However, every time we needed to leave, it seemed as though someone was opening up a valve at the headwaters of the river that caused the river to rise. Not once did the river fail to rise when we needed to leave.

One day, Ruth was teaching the women to sew, showing them how to operate the sewing machine. Isidora was sitting at the machine. She was tense. As she operated the pedal that caused the machine to sew, it would run backwards and cut the thread. Ruth would re-thread the needle, and Isidora would try again. It took many tries before she learned to operate the machine. Eventually, all the women learned to sew. Ruth cut out patterns for all the men, women, and children in the village. By cutting out the materials from the patterns, they now could make their own clothes.

*Ruth joins Orejon women Isidora and Griselda for a photo.*

Ruth had asked Gustavo to clear a patch of ground just below the village so she could plant a garden. Gustavo was clearing the land as Ruth was teaching the women to sew and I was teaching some of the men the Spanish numbering system.

The Señora was able to cheat the people because they didn't know Spanish and didn't know the numbering system, nor the value of the Peruvian sol.

She claimed to own the Indians and could make them do anything she wanted. One time, she borrowed my 36-foot canoe, loaded it with plantains, cassava roots, and wild pig skins to take to Iquitos to sell. I estimated she received about 3,000 soles for the entire lot. She paid them with five bottles of cane whiskey, and three liter bottles of kerosene—worth about five soles.

*Ruth and Bob stand in front of their new house in the village.*

– 14 –

# Gustavo and the Snakebite

Gustavo had been working about an hour when he came to the house saying he had been bitten by a shushupi, a very poisonous snake.

I cranked up the generator and called the doctor at Yarina Cocha, our base. "If you have ice, put an ice pack on the wound. Keep ice on it for at least four hours. The body will build its own anti-venom. Don't lance the wound. People die from infections more than the venom."

By this time, we had been living in the village for a long period of time and had been able to purchase a small two-cubic-foot kerosene refrigerator. It had two small ice trays that gave us ice twice a day. When the Indians brought us wild meat, we would keep it in the refrigerator.

The Indians had not been hunting for several days and were out of meat. Ruth was cooking a roast from a wild peccary. One of the men asked, "Where did you get the meat?"

I showed him the refrigerator and had him put his hand inside. Several had by now gathered, so I took out small cubes of ice and handed each one.

"Cold," they said as they tossed the cube from hand

to hand. I then showed them the burning flame at the bottom of the refrigerator. "How can fire make something so cold?" Another mystery to them.

I had Gustavo sit down so I could see the fang pricks. There were two on his ankle. Ruth made two bags from cloth to hold the ice.

As soon as I put one bag of ice on the wound and the ice melted, Ruth would bring me the other. We kept this up for at least five hours. The refrigerator kept making ice, but when the swelling went down, it wouldn't make any more ice. I gave Gustavo an injection of antibiotic and told him to lie down with his leg elevated, and then I left.

The next day, we tried getting the machine to make more ice. It wouldn't. How does one explain this? Only God could keep the ice coming as long as we needed it. Matthew 6 again.

I checked later, and his ankle was looking good. I gave him another injection of antibiotic.

The next morning, I checked on Gustavo. He was sitting up, looking as if he had lost his last friend. I asked him what was wrong, and he showed me his ankle. It was wrapped in a dirty rag with some green-looking paste.

I asked, "Who put that on your ankle?"

"The witch doctor is treating me," he responded.

"The ankle is swelling again. Do you want the witch doctor to treat you, or do you want me?" I asked.

"I want you to treat me," he responded.

"If you want me to treat you, fine. But you can't have the witch doctor treat you."

The witch doctor saw an opportunity to take credit for curing a shushupi bite. We were told no one ever survived a shushupi bite.

From then on, the witch doctor avoided me, but Gustavo's ankle healed completely.

Sometime later, I don't remember why I was at the village alone, but Ruth was at Yarina Cocha. One morning, the Señora showed up. Her son Herman had brought her.

"I want you to go upriver and bring me all the peccary (wild pig) skins you can kill" was her order the moment she stepped into their main hut, a large grass-covered, open-air building where they all usually gathered. "I will give each of you ten shotgun shells. I expect a skin for every shell you use. I will go with you."

Ruth was not on this trip. The Señora knew I would accompany them on this trip, and she wanted to control who took the skins to Iquitos.

Two days upriver was their hunting ground teeming with wild pigs. The first day, we made it halfway and had to make camp on the bank of the river. I took one of our jungle hammocks and found two sturdy trees on which to sling it. This time I planned to eat with the Indians, so I didn't take along any cans of food.

The next afternoon, we arrived at the hut they had constructed on a previous trip. Grass had grown high, but with their machetes, they made short work of clearing the area. The women swept the floor and made the place livable.

The men went immediately hunting and came back

with several pigs. They shared the meat with me along with cassava roots they had planted on the last trip.

Isidora complained of stomach pains, so the Señora had her lie down. Where they wouldn't see her, she slipped a chunk of tobacco into her mouth. Next, she began sucking on her stomach, raised up, and spit out a large wad of black-looking gunk. "Look what I sucked from your stomach—that was why your stomach hurt."

Isidora didn't know that she had been tricked. She trusted the Señora. Hadn't she taken care of them all these years?

We had been there several days, and the Indians had killed a lot of pigs. Pig skins were standing on frames, drying, on every available spot, and meat was being smoked on open fires.

We had lived with them long enough to gain their trust. I asked Miguel, "Would you like me to take you, with your meat and skins, to Iquitos to sell, and give you the money to let you purchase things for yourself, instead of letting the Señora give you very little, like she always has?"

"I would like that" was his instant reply. Their word for I like is "deu."

After a few days of hunting and smoking the meat, they had enough to fill both canoes, their canoe and mine. It took us a day and a half to get to the hunting area, but only a little more than half a day to get back. There was lots of water in the river, so it flowed quite rapidly, and we made good time. Besides, there were not any trees across the river that had to be cut through.

The Indians took their meat and skins to the Señora, except Miguel. She let them keep some of the smoked meat for themselves. Miguel was able to keep all of his to eat.

Early the next morning, Miguel, Hoya, and I loaded Miguel's skins and meat into my 36-foot canoe and headed down the Sucusari river and onto the Napo River. I only had the two-horsepower Penta that Ruth likened to an egg beater. It didn't push the canoe very fast, so we only made it halfway up the Amazon river to Iquitos. We stopped at a typical house—thatch roof and poles. No walls. We were given permission to spend the night. It began to rain—I mean really rain. Although we had the meat and skins covered, Miguel sat up all night bailing out the canoe.

We arrived in Iquitos about two in the afternoon, and Miguel and Hoya carried the meat and skins to a warehouse that purchased both skins and meat. After weighing the meat and counting the skins, the man paid Miguel several hundred soles.

"What do you want to buy with your money?" I asked Miguel.

"I want a shotgun and shells." The shotguns the Indians were using belonged to the Señora, so she told them.

"I also want a pair of shoes."

"First," I said, "we need to have something to eat. I know of a restaurant that serves good food at a low price." It was a communal house that served the poor.

Miguel had never used a knife, fork, and spoon before, so I had to teach him. "Hay que aprender," he responded, which translated into Spanish as, "One must learn."

After eating, we went shopping. With his money, he purchased a new shotgun and a box of shells. Next, he purchased a store-made dress for Maria, several bolts of cloth—for which he chose the colors—and a pair of shoes for himself.

As I watched him walking down the street, it looked as though he was walking on stilts. Finally, he took the shoes off and tucked them under his arm. When we got back to the village, he tied the shoes to the rafter above his sleeping area for all to see: "Look, I have shoes."

When we got back to the village and the people could see what Miguel had purchased with his money, and compare that with what the Señora had given them, they could see she was cheating them.

This was the straw that finally broke the hold the Señora had over them.

*Miguel and Hoya ride the Sucusari River at low water.*

— 15 —

# The Velies Replace Us

Not long after, Ruth arrived back at the village. We were closing up our time with them. I gave them the outboard motor so they could take their own produce to Iquitos. Romero was well into Spanish, so he could be their spokesman.

Dan and Virginia Velie were living at Yarina Cocha, waiting for an opportunity to serve in a tribal area.

We didn't feel we could leave the tribe alone without someone looking out for their welfare, so we asked if someone could come and replace us.

Uncle Cam, the director, asked Dan and Virginia if they would be in agreement to take over. They agreed.

Dan and Virginia moved into our house, which came complete with kitchen cabinets, a bed, and the two-cubic-foot refrigerator.

Several months earlier, I had taken Romero to Yarina and taught him to read Spanish. He was a very mentally alert young man and learned very rapidly. On our return to the village, we stopped in Iquitos for supplies. We walked past a store with a sign that read, "Casa Romero." He stopped, looked at the sign, and said, "That's my name." He was so pleased he could read.

I suppose God had chosen us to open up the tribe to the Gospel. We didn't get any translation done, but Dan was given free reign to work. The Señora no longer had control of the tribe, so she did not bother Dan or Virginia. They were able to live in the tribe and dedicate their time to translating the Bible into the Orejon language.

# FURLOUGH

## — 16 —

# *We Bought a House*

We had been in Peru for more than five years, so it was time for us to return to the U.S. We arrived in the States about July 1958. Because we had sold our triplex to pay our way to Peru, we no longer had a home in Seattle.

Ruth was getting very good at packing, so she started in again. At one point, Ruth counted we had moved 26 times. We first lived with Ruth's parents at Trinity Bay, Texas; then moved to Seattle; and through our church, received an offer to spend the winter at Sammamish Bible Camp in the original old two-story house on the campus.

We moved into the Lake Sammamish house, and no sooner had we moved in than Ruth called an adoption agency. A fertility doctor in Peru informed us that for us to have our own children would not be very likely.

We learned that Washington State planned on building a freeway through Seattle and, through the process of eminent domain, was selling houses that stood in the way of the freeway expansion.

We also heard the houses were being sold just to get them off the lots for the needed freeway, so bids were accepted as low as $100.

We offered a bid of $100 for a house we had chosen, and it was accepted. I later learned they would have accepted $50, but the houses had to be removed by a certain date. We now owned a house, but where would we put it? At the time, Romans 8:28 hadn't crossed our minds; we just wanted our own house, and this appeared our best option to get one.

Next, I contacted a realtor about buying a lot on which to put the house. We were shown several lots and chose one in our price range.

Our next project was contacting a house mover to move the house from where it sat on the proposed freeway to our lot in the north end of Seattle.

"I'm sorry, but we are so booked up, I doubt we can get it moved in time to avoid the huge penalty the State will charge for every day the move is delayed" was what every mover told us.

The next Sunday after church, I told our pastor the bad news. He went into his office and made a phone call. "I just called a friend who moves houses, and as a favor to me, he agreed to move your house for you." Romans 8:28 came to mind. Is God making "all things work together for good" once again? Is God that interested in the little things in our lives that would alter our lives to this extent? Was it just an accident that our pastor knew a mover who could come to our aid when others were not that fortunate? A man who was going to make a huge profit bought six houses. His problem? He couldn't find a mover and lost his financial shirt.

We ran into another problem. The mover called and said, "The roof is too tall to move the house without taking off the roof. To move the house with the existing roof will cost a considerable amount for the power company to cut the power lines across the street. And there are a lot of them. If you will take the existing roof off, we can move the house without having to cut the power lines."

I contacted a man from our church who agreed to help me remove the roof. We were told that the State would remove the boards and roofing left after the roof was removed.

We began early the next morning and worked hard all that day and the next. The second day, the man who had bought the six houses came and asked if we would help him tear off his roofs.

"I'm sorry, but we don't have time because our house mover is coming to move our house, and we have to get my roof off. We would be happy to help, but we just don't have the time." Besides, we had worked long hours the past two days, and we were tired.

When I arrived home that evening, Ruth met me at the door and said, "Guess who called today?"

"Who?" I asked.

"The lady from the adoption agency called. They have a brother and sister who need a home," Ruth said.

"How old are they" was my next question.

"The girl is two years old, and the boy three. I said we'd take both of them. Are you OK with that?" Ruth questioned.

"Yeah, I guess so. What are their names?"

"The girl's name is Marilyn, and the boy is Richard. The lady said she would get back to us."

Two days later, the movers arrived, placed the house onto the huge dolly, and slowly pulled the house the three miles to its new location. Then they moved the house from the dolly onto the cribbing that was placed over the hole for the basement.

A few days later, the agency called back and said, "Because you two are willing to take both children, we are considering you. However, a problem has arisen. The family that has been taking care of the girl wants to adopt her and is willing to go to court to get her. We will call you after we know just what is going to happen. We don't think the court will separate the two because they are brother and sister, but we won't know until after the hearing.

A long period of time elapsed with no word about the children. We had about given up hope, thinking that having children was not in God's will.

I kept commuting back and forth, working on the house. There were lots of things that had to be done before we could call the place home. A basement and floor had to be poured.

I learned of a Christian who did concrete work. I was given his phone number and called him.

"Hello, this is Sam, what can I do for you?"

"I just purchased a freeway house, and I need someone to pour a basement. Do you do that kind of work?"

"Where is your house located?"

"It's in Lake City."

I gave him the address, and he said, "I'll come out and look at it and decide if I want to do it."

I met him at the house at the agreed time. He walked around the house and finally said, "I can do it. Do I need to hire someone, or will you work with me?"

The next morning he gave me a list of the lumber I would need and said he would be back as soon as the lumber was delivered.

I immediately drove to the lumber yard and put in my order.

"We can deliver the lumber by noon tomorrow."

I called Sam, and he said he would be at my house in the morning. He arrived by eight and about worked me to death. Besides being a large man, he worked me harder than I have ever worked in my life. By the end of the day, I was more tired than I have ever been.

By the end of the second day, the forms were all in and ready for the cement truck. Before we left, I called the concrete company and ordered the cement. They said they would be at the house by ten the next morning. Sam and I met the truck, and the pouring began, with Sam directing. Sam placed anchor bolts into the wet cement walls for anchoring the plates on which to place to house.

Two days later, Sam and I removed the wooden frame from the concrete walls. The time had finally come to lower the house onto the new foundation.

We then received a call from the Wycliffe office, asking us to represent Wycliffe at a Missionary Conference in

Spokane. We agreed to do that, so we packed up all our novelties we had brought from Peru, including the nineteen-foot boa constrictor skin. Yes, I killed the boa that was too near our village, and I brought the skin home and had it tanned at a tannery in Fremont, a suburb in the north end of Seattle. I also took the seven-foot blowgun and darts the Indians used to kill small birds and monkeys, a large canoe paddle, plus a few other items that made up the life of the Indians.

After our three-day conference, we returned to Seattle only to find a heavy wind and rainstorm had torn much of the tar paper off the roof, and the oak floors were damaged. They were all curled up and appeared ruined, and the ceiling plasterboard was ruined.

An older man from church who was familiar with oak flooring said, "Bob, you can't ruin oak floors. Just nail the boards back down, have the floor sanded, and you won't be able to tell they were damaged."

We did just that, and sure enough, they looked new and beautiful.

## — 17 —

## *We Become Parents*

After having almost given up on the adoption, we got a call from the adoption agency. "We won the court case! The judge didn't want the two separated, so we are awarding the children to you. However, we suggest you change their names."

"We would like for you to meet the children," the case worker said. "Could you be here on Tuesday to spend some time with them?"

*Ruth and her new children, Kevin and Jana, enjoy a walk around town.*

"Of course we can."

After meeting at the agency, we went to the park, spent a couple of hours with the children, and had a wonderful time together.

As we left the children, Ruth commented, "It looks as though God is giving us children in spite of what the doctor in Peru said. I know he said we couldn't have children the normal way, but this is the next best thing."

March 9, 1959, while we were still living in the old farmhouse, two adorable children, Richard and Marilyn, came to share our home. Having been asked to change their names, we chose Kevin for Richard and Jana for Marilyn.

A short time later, we were asked to vacate the farmhouse at Sammamish because it would be needed for camp-related activities.

A friend, who owned several apartments, and whose wife had recently passed away, offered to let us move into his apartment located in Seattle. This meant I no longer had to commute the long distance from Sammamish to work on the house.

Our church held a baby shower for the two children. They were given lots of clothing, toys, and a new tricycle each.

With the help of many from our church, the house was completed enough for us to move in, with temporary wooden steps leading into the living room. Friends from the church donated furniture, and a man who owned a furnace company installed an oil tank and oil furnace, complete with a thermostat.

We had no sooner gotten settled in the house than the agency called and said they wanted to visit us and the children to see how we were doing.

Ruth answered the phone and said, "Why don't you have dinner with us tonight?"

In the course of the dinner, the lady made an observation. As she observed the house, which was unfinished, with temporary steps and no lawn, she commented, "I don't understand why we awarded the children to you, with you living in an unfinished house, with no steady job, and planning to take the children out of the country. It just doesn't make sense to me."

She didn't know we have a God who works things out in His own way, His wonders to perform.

We were now a complete, happy family living pretty normal lives. Members of our church and I kept working on the house, finishing up the loose ends. One day, friends from the church came and put in a front lawn, complete with shrubs, and the men built a carport next to the house.

Doing hard work on the house was good for my health. When we came home from Peru in 1958, I had jungle sores on my legs that took a long time to heal. After living with the Indians, eating with them, and being on duty seven days a week, 24 hours every day, I had intestinal parasites that the doctors treated. It took two years for me to recuperate.

Besides working on the house, we were available to represent Wycliffe at churches and conferences, but in 1960, the Wycliffe office contacted us, asking if we would be able to return to Peru for me to take over the buyer's office in Lima. We said we were ready to return to Peru. That meant once again leaving a nice home we had worked so hard to finish.

Wednesday evening, we attended a Bible study and prayer meeting at our church, where the members told us goodbye. Several walked with us to the car. As I approached the car, I noticed the trunk was open and the spare tire was gone.

"Look, the spare tire is gone. Now we will have more room for luggage," I said.

The Chairman of the church board responded, "That's not faith—that's presumption."

# BACK TO PERU

## — 18 —

## Living in Lima

The next morning, as we were packing, a member came over and said, "Let me take care of your house while you are gone. I'll see that it is rented, and I'll take care of any maintenance it needs."

I told Selmer how much I appreciated that and that he could take expenses from the rent.

"No, I won't charge you anything; it will be part of my ministry."

After Ruth got the little Studebaker Champion packed (she is really good at packing), we headed out.

I believe the Studebaker was a 1950 model that Ruth's brother loaned us, but it ran very well. We were traveling through Arizona. The weather was scorching—with no air-conditioning. In 1960, there were not many service stations. We were getting low on gasoline, so at the first station we came to, we stopped. Just as I pulled into the station, we heard a shshshsh sound. The left rear tire went flat.

Have I ever made any mistakes? Yes, and this was a biggy. If the tire had gone flat out in the middle of nowhere, what would I have done? I didn't have a spare tire, nor a jack, nor a lug wrench. I would have had to leave Ruth and the children in the boiling hot sun while I hitched a ride into the next town, then hitched a ride back.

With no shade trees, no air-conditioning, and 120-degree heat, they could have ended up with heat stroke.

God must have laughed at my stupidity, but He kept air in that tire until we arrived at a service station. Since then, I have tried to be a bit wiser.

If you have read our story, I hope you can look back at your life and recognize God's hand guiding your life.

Another translation of Proverbs 3:5–6 reads, "Trust in the Lord with all your heart, and don't lean on your own understanding, but in ALL your ways acknowledge Him, and He will make your paths straight."

We were again met at the Lima airport by Mrs. Cudney, who handed Ruth a bouquet of beautiful flowers, looked at Kevin and Jana, and responded, "So these are the children you adopted." She knelt down and gave each a hug, saying, "Welcome to Lima. We have a room all ready for you. I'll bet you are all hungry."

We followed Mrs. Cudney to pick up our luggage and then followed her to the station wagon and on to the group home.

In a few days, we located a house we could afford, and an American nurse friend, who worked at the British-American hospital, acquired furniture from a family who was leaving Peru.

As soon as we moved in, I began work in the office. There were three Peruvians working, buying and shipping to Yarina, when I took over. It took three men full-time to do all the buying. Lima was a driver's nightmare. Lima kept importing more and more cars, but they didn't do anything to improve the traffic. The streets were no more than a slow-moving parking lot.

To solve that problem, I purchased a German Zundap motorcycle and fitted a box on the back. I could go around or between the cars or drive on the sidewalk.

I could do the buying much faster, so I released two of the boys. I did keep Juan Huamani to help me, a fine Christian.

A tribe living in the mountains near Cuzco built cement troughs across the river. When the river rose during a storm, the water carried gold down the mountain and deposited it behind the cement troughs. When the river receded, the Indians would collect the gold, and the translator, Bob Tripp, would weigh the gold and write down the owner's name. He would then send the gold to the buyer in Lima. The previous buyer would take the gold to a gold buyer, sell it to him, then deposit the amount in Bob's account. Bob would distribute the money among the tribal members.

I saw no sense in letting the gold buyer make the profit from the gold, so I located the State's smelting room, a large room in a run-down old building. I talked with the man in charge, and he said I could bring the gold to him and he would smelt the gold into bars and assay the gold to determine the percent of copper and other materials contained in the gold.

I could then take the gold bar to a bank and get the

highest price—which I did. Bob's tribe got a lot more money for their gold.

It was interesting to watch the man pour the gold sand or dust (or whatever it is called), into a cast-iron caldron (melting pot), pour borax over the gold, and turn on the fire. The impurities would float to the top and stick to the borax. When the gold cooled, the borax that now contained the impurities was peeled off and thrown away. The gold was then put in a sink and brushed with a wire brush. Then a small hole was drilled into the gold, and the gold filings were assayed to determine the percent of pure gold. Ours was 99.6 percent pure gold.

After nearly two years as buyer, I was asked to go to Yarina Cocha to become the overseer of the Publications Department. That meant another packing up and moving to Yarina. Then another miracle happened.

– 19 –

## Barbara is Born

Ruth complained about not feeling well, so she went to Dr. Kruger, a German who had fled Bolivia and settled in Lima. When she came home from the hospital, she announced, "Want to know a secret? I'm pregnant." Five months before we moved to Yarina, Barbara was born, a beautiful little girl. Kevin and Jana were attending a Peruvian school. Kevin became the best friend of an American girl in his class. Her name was Barbara. Just the week before, her father had taken the family in a small plane to take pictures of the majestic Andes Mountains. With one hand, he had piloted the plane, and with the other hand, he had held the camera. He made a terrible mistake that cost the lives of his entire family. The plane plunged into a mountain, and all were killed.

Kevin was devastated. He cried for days. When Barbara was born, Kevin asked if we could name his new sister Barbara.

We liked the name, so that was our new baby's name. Five months after Barbara was born, Ruth had, once again, to pack everything for our move to Yarina. I had to remain in Lima to train another Wycliffe member to take over as the new buyer. I was so busy that I didn't have much time to be with the family nor to hold my new daughter very much.

Ruth had moved into a house belonging to a family that was home on furlough. When I finally did get to Yarina and picked up my new daughter, she remembered who I was, her daddy. She wouldn't let me put her down.

– 20 –

# The Yarina Cocha Print Shop

I shipped my motorcycle to Yarina. I don't know whether the new buyer bought himself a motorcycle or if the group provided one for him. I never did ask.

Barbara loved to ride on my motorcycle. When I started for work, Barbara would fuss until I gave her a short ride on my motorcycle. Then she was happy.

About five months after we arrived at Yarina, Barbara became very ill. She wouldn't eat and had constant diarrhea and fever.

The doctors at the base put her on antibiotics—so much that the antibiotics killed all the good and bad bacteria in her body.

Doctor Kruger from Lima, who had diagnosed Ruth's pregnancy, came out to the base for some R-and-R. He was walking toward the clinic at the same time as Ruth, who was carrying Barbara. As he looked at Barbara, he asked Ruth, "What's wrong with Barbara?"

Ruth explained the problems that Barbara was having: constant diarrhea, fever, and she wouldn't eat. Dr. Kruger met with both base doctors, and after much discussion, he told the doctors he would take over Barbara. Before he came to the base, he had announced that he was there for a vacation and would not be seeing any patients.

From the day he delivered Barbara, he loved her like his own. Even with a room full of patients waiting to see him, if Ruth walked into his office waiting room, he would take Barbara in his arms, go out to his garden behind his clinic, and show her all his exotic shrubs and plants.

At the base, Dr. Kruger gave Barbara a shot of something. When he returned to Lima, he sent some medicines he had purchased from Germany. I think some was to replace the good bacteria the antibiotics had destroyed. Anyway, Barbara got better, but it was suggested we return to the States, where she could get better treatment.

*In Aeronca planes, we fly over the Wycliffe base at Yarina Cocha.*

The climate in Lima is very dry, but the climate in the jungle is very humid. There are four seasons in the jungle: hot, hotter, wet, and wetter.

I enjoyed being in charge of the print shop, but I wasn't that essential. The Orejons were well taken care of, the buyer in Lima was doing a good job, and there was another Wycliffe member who could take over managing the print shop.

The only change I made in the print shop was in the development of black-and-white films. The previous manager had sent all black-and-white films to Lima for processing. As a teenager, I had dabbled in photography. I had learned to develop films and print copies.

A pilot on base knew photography, so I asked Jim Price if he would be willing to teach a Peruvian to develop and process the films that the translators sent to be processed.

"I'd be happy to train someone" was his instant reply.

I sent to Lima a list of the equipment Jim made out, and before long, we were in business. Now the films could be processed almost immediately and at a much lower cost. The Davidson press was operated by a Peruvian who was doing a wonderful job. There were professional artists who drew pictures for the primers sent in by the linguists. Everything was moving along very nicely.

Ruth, again, began sorting out our belongings and getting ready to sell what we couldn't take with us. Soon we were on our way to the States. Jeremiah 29:11 says, "For I know the plans that I have for you, declares the Lord..."

*The family, now complete, poses in Yarina Cocha shortly before returning to the States.*

# BACK TO THE U.S.

## — 21 —

## *Registering at the University of Washington*

This time, we had a house in Seattle where we could live. We had resigned from Wycliffe, but what course should we take now? I had always wanted to be a teacher, so I talked to Ruth about my going back to college and getting a teaching certificate. We had very little money, but we knew God would provide.

I decided to go to the University of Washington and see if I would be accepted. I was past 40 years of age. First, I had to fill out a formal questionnaire.

Dr. Briggs was assigned as my counselor. As we sat down, he looked at my application and said, "Bob, there are three things against you. Number one: your age is against you. You haven't been in a classroom for several years. You are not used to studying, especially competing with kids who have spent their entire lives studying. Number two: the University costs money I'm not sure you have. And three: there are no teaching positions available with the economy as it is."

"I know this sounds a bit grim, but, Dr. Briggs, if God told me to walk through that wall, it would be my responsibility to start walking and God's responsibility to make a hole."

Dr. Briggs laughed and responded, "With your attitude like that, I can't refuse you. You are ready to go."

I thanked him and started a new chapter in our lives. I wanted Ruth at home with the kids and didn't want her working outside the home. I didn't want some stranger taking care of them. We trusted God to take care of us, just has He had always done.

As we look back, we can't figure out how God did take care of us. After a year and a half, when I received my Certificate, we didn't owe anyone, and all our bills were paid, including our utility bills. During the month I did have off between quarters in the summer, I put an ad in the newspaper—"Flat Roof Specialist"—and gave my telephone number. I had never done a tar roof in my life, but I knew I could do it. I had done everything else.

From the garbage dump, I found a 15-gallon oil drum and a burner from a gas furnace. I made a tar pot and with the gas burner from a discarded gas furnace, I was in business. I purchased a 32-foot ladder. The work was hard because I had to carry the melted tar in five-gallon buckets onto the roof.

I immediately received calls from my ad. I could make $100 per day by working eight or more hours repairing leaking roofs. The work was hard, but it was rewarding. Along with the tar roofs, I got several carpentry jobs.

As we look back, we can't see how God made our money s t r e t c h, but He did.

*The Year of Abundance—we canned 78 quarts of string beans in one day!*

Ruth planted a garden as she has always done, but this garden was different. During the summer, Ruth was able to can 78 quarts of string beans all in one day, and we had an ample supply of the other vegetables she had planted.

Also, Ruth is a professional seamstress, so she made all the clothes for herself and the children.

The last month I attended the University, I was assigned to do my Student Teaching at Ingram High School. My supervising teacher was Gill Koller.

About two weeks into my teaching assignment, the head of the Business Department of the Seattle Schools called Gill and asked him how I was doing.

Gill responded, "He's doing fine."

"Do you think he will make a good teacher?"

"He's only been here two weeks."

"At this point, do you feel he will be a good teacher, able to fit into the Seattle schools?"

"I would say, yes, he will do very well as a teacher. He knows his subjects, and I would recommend him."

"Have him drop by my office when he has some time free to do so."

I called his office and made an appointment to meet with him. When I showed up, we just chatted. Nothing was mentioned about a job. I was somewhat puzzled as to why he wanted to talk with me.

Just before I was finished with my Student Teaching assignment, all Student Teachers were requested to be at a teachers' meeting at Nathan Hale High School.

The Director was walking ahead of me, but he dropped back and said, "I think we are going to hire you. Drop by my office."

The next day, I did stop at his office. Without saying more than a greeting, he shoved a contract in front of me and said, "Sign here. I am assigning you to teach typing and a special class we are forming for disadvantaged young people. We want you to teach that class. There aren't any teaching plans for that particular subject, but we want you prepare these children to be able to function on their own in the outside world."

"You want me to prepare these young people to apply for a job, to manage finances, and to conduct themselves in a working environment?"

"Exactly. Do you think you can do it?"

"I know I can," was my instant reply.

That was my most rewarding class. It was a fun class. I made up checks just like they would get from a job. They learned how to make a budget, how to make out a bank deposit slip, how to calculate how much they could spend for items they would have to buy, and how to keep their budget within the amount they deposited in the bank.

Over the course of the quarter, they learned how to function on their own.

I was able to relate to these students because I was brought up in the same environment. My dad pounded into me that I would never amount to anything, that I was dumb. He was quick to let me know when I did something wrong but never complimented me when I did something right. These young people had the same experiences.

I determined that I would work on their self-esteem. I made sure they succeeded and complimented each as he or she did.

I looked back at what Dr. Briggs told me, "There are no teaching jobs available." Dr. Briggs didn't know God already had a plan for my life. I didn't even fill out an application. God works in mysterious ways, His wonders to perform.

One day, Sally raised her hand.

"What is it, Sally?" I asked.

"You know why my mom won't let my dad go to Hawaii?"

"No, why?"

"Cause my dad has so many children in Hawaii, one of the women might recognize him." The children had no inhibitions about anything.

Sally was earning a C-average grade. One day, I asked her, "Sally, why don't you try for a B average?"

"Mr. Sandberg, what's wrong with a C grade? My counselor told me I would never make higher than a C."

"Why don't you try for a B," I suggested.

Sometime later, she got a paper with an 85 percent, which was a B. Sally was elated. From then on, she worked harder to earn more B's.

To be closer to home, I asked for a transfer to a Business teaching job that had opened up at Nathan Hale High School, and it was granted.

I lost track of my "special students" after my transfer. But several years later, I was at Providence Hospital. While waiting my turn to see a doctor, a young woman passed. It was Dorothy. I called her name, and she turned around. When she first came to my class, she was very sullen and would hardly look at me. She wouldn't smile.

As she turned around, a big smile spread across her face. She said, "Hello, Mr. Sandberg." I got up and gave her a big hug, then she told me, "I have a good job and my own apartment, and I'm living on my own."

She was working as an assistant to a nurse.

Sometime later, I met Robert at a mall. He told me he had graduated from the University of Washington and had earned a Masters Degree.

When he came to my class, he had a defeatist attitude. His father had drilled into him just what my dad had drilled into me—that he would never amount to anything.

These two students made my day.

Dr. Briggs didn't know that God had my life all planned out. But He did.

# CONCLUSION

There are many more miracles in our 64 years together, but if what we have written will not convince you that Proverbs 3:5-6 is true—"Trust wholeheartedly in Yahweh, put no faith in your own perception; in every course you take, have Him in mind: He will see that your paths are smooth" (The Jerusalem Bible)—if it will not convince you that there is a God, then nothing will.

Although I didn't know anything about the Bible, I learned very early in life that when we die, we don't take anything with us. Luke 12:15 states, "Watch, and be on your guard against avarice [greed] of any kind, for a man's life is not made secure by what he owns"(The Jerusalem Bible).

I saw this as I looked into caskets. I thought, "What's the purpose of working hard all one's life to just leave it all behind for someone to fight over?"

Over the years, I have heard people complain, "I pray and nothing happens." Others have said, "Where was God when I needed him?" Still others said, "I don't believe the Bible; it's just a myth." Many have said to me, "There are so many religions, which ones should we believe? So I don't believe any of them."

If I mention the scripture in Hebrew 9:27—"And inas-much as it is appointed for men to die once and after this comes judgment."—they either don't respond, or they say they will take their chances.

I am sure we, as a "modern" culture, have our wants and needs mixed up. We are told by TV and radio that our lives are not complete until we purchase the item or items they sell. We deserve all these things, and we can't be happy until we have them. So we go into debt, then ask God to help us pay our bills.

Paul wrote to the Philippian church that he knew how to be poor and rich too. Read Paul's letter to the Philippian church—Philippians chapter 4, verse 20: "In return my God will fulfill all your NEEDS, in Christ Jesus, as lavishly as only God can" (The Jerusalem Bible). He didn't say "all your wants," only your needs.

Matthew 6:8 says, "...for your Father knows what you need, before you ask Him." Does this mean we don't need to pray because God already knows what we need?

In Luke 22:40, Jesus commands his disciples to "pray that you may not enter into temptation."

Matthew 6:6 says, "But when you pray, go into your inner room, and when you have shut your door, pray to your Father who is in secret, and your Father who sees in secret will repay you."

And Matthew 5:44 states, "But I say to you, love your enemies, and pray for those who persecute you."

There are many verses on prayer, and this is only a sample. The Bible has many more verses on prayer.

For most of us, God has given us sound minds and

strong bodies. If we want something, we have the mind and body to work for the luxury items we feel we have to have.

As an affluent country, we can't seem to be content with what we have—we are a people who want more. Ruth and I have never worked for wealth. We can't take it with us. Dust we are, and to dust we will return. We have striven to make a difference in the lives of others, that we will leave this earth better than it was when we came here.

Have we made mistakes, done "dumb" things? Of course, but God has a way of making even bad choices come out OK.

The story of the missing spare tire is a good example of just one mistake I (Bob) have made.

"My little children, I am writing these things to you that you may not sin. But if anyone does sin, we have an advocate with the Father: Jesus Christ the righteous" (1 John 2:1).

I do not want to leave you with the impression that God is against wealth. 2 Chronicles 1:7–12 says:

> In that night God appeared to Solomon and said to him, "Ask what I shall give you."
>
> And Solomon said to God, "Thou hast dealt with my father David with great lovingkindness, and hast made me king in this place.
>
> "Now, O Lord God, Thy promise to my father David is fulfilled; for Thou hast made me king over a people as numerous as the dust of the earth. Give me wisdom and knowledge that I may go out and come in before this people; for who can rule this great people of Thine?"

*And God said to Solomon, "Because you have had this in mind, and did not ask for riches, wealth, or honor, or the life of those who hate you, nor have you even asked for long life, but you have asked for yourself wisdom and knowledge, that you may rule My people, over whom I have made you king, wisdom and knowledge have been granted you. And I will give you riches and wealth and honor, such as none of the kings who were before you has possessed, nor those who will come after you."*

My own thought: I think all that wealth and honor went to Solomon's head. Could that happen to you?

May God bless your life as you continue to walk with Him and seek His daily guidance.

LaVergne, TN USA
26 January 2011
214128LV00001B/5/P